Ireland's Largest Industrial Railway
The Guinness System
Hugh Oram

Two narrow gauge locos – one steam (left), he other diesel – outside the Robert Street maltstore in 1948. The diesel loco is hauling a train of hop wagons.

1

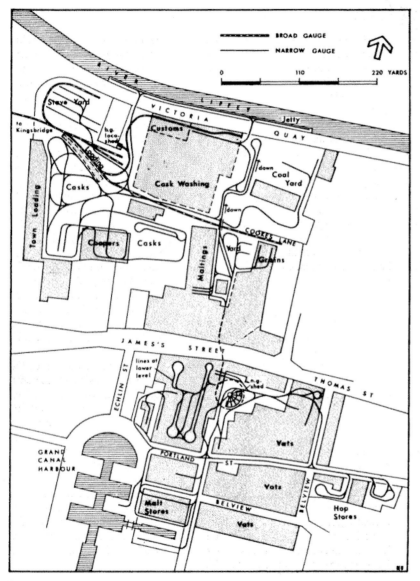

Acknowledgements

I'd like to thank my wife Bernadette for all her encouragement and also Thelma Byrne, Aisling Curley, Maria Gillen, Ellen Monnelly and Mary J. Murphy for the support they gave me during the production of this book. I'd like to give particular acknowledgement to Eibhlin Colgan, the Guinness archivist, Tim Moriarty and Clifton Flewitt of the Irish Railway Record Society at Heuston station, Dublin, Andrew Waldron of the Industrial Railway Society, David Laing of Herbertson Art & Collectibles, Nuneaton, and Paul Webb.

Above all, I'd like to thank Michael McMahon of Collon, Co. Louth, to whom I owe a debt of gratitude for fact checking the copy and supplying extra material about the Guinness tramway. Other thanks go to Rachel Spiller, Amberley Museum and Railway Centre, Arundel, West Sussex, Eddie Byrne, Gay Byrne, Nick Fairall, Guinness Collectors' Club, Tom Ferris, Wales, John Giles and Rob Goodbody, Industrial Heritage Association, Robert C. Guinness of the Straffan Steam Museum, Co. Kildare, Mark Kennedy, Ulster Folk & Transport Museum, Co. Down, Michael Kennedy, Irish Narrow Gauge Trust/Cavan & Leitrim Railway Museum, Co. Leitrim, Paul McCann, Railway Preservation Society of Ireland, Co. Antrim, National Library of Ireland, Don Newing, Narrow Gauge Railway Museum, Wales, Alan O' Rourke, Hassard Stacpoole and Jonathan Virden (Guinness brewer, 1961–1973) .

The photographs were supplied by the Guinness Archives and by Andrew Waldron of the Industrial Railway Society.

This 1960 map illustrates the layout of the narrow gauge system.

Introduction

The Guinness brewery in Dublin had a remarkable narrow gauge railway, or more properly, tramway, within the brewery itself, as well as a broad gauge link to the nearby goods yard at what was then Kingsbridge station, now Heuston. Construction of the railway started in 1873 and the narrow gauge part of the system was closed down in 1975, ten years after the broad gauge link.

In the early 1870s Guinness had embarked on a major expansion plan, which included the purchase of much land adjacent to Victoria Quay on the River Liffey. At that stage the brewery was expanding so fast that Guinness was able to promote itself as the largest brewery in the world. Until then the brewery had used horse-drawn carts around the brewery to haul loads such as hops, malt and casks, but the expansion meant that a new system of transport was needed. The right man came along at the right time: Samuel Geoghegan, a very inventive engineer with much experience outside Ireland, including on the railways in India.

In 1872, at the age of 28, he joined the staff of the Guinness engineering department and was involved with both the planning of the railway and its construction. By 1875 he was chief engineer and he spent the rest of his career prospering at Guinness, living at No. 21 Ailesbury Road, then as now one of the most exclusive addresses in Dublin. He retired in 1905, aged 61, and died in 1928. His brother, William Purser Geoghegan, also did well at Guinness, becoming the head brewer in 1880.

Malt wagons outside the No. 2 brewery, 1920.

Samuel Geoghegan was a remarkably inventive man and put this skill to use in solving problems that arose with the railway. The first problem came with the steam locomotives, half a dozen in all, purchased from English makers. The earliest locos didn't perform well; one of their inadequacies was the difficulty of keeping dirt out of the engine motion. So Geoghegan set about designing a steam locomotive that overcame these faults and he found a local foundry and engineering company that was willing to build it, despite the lack of any experience in this area.

This was William Spence and Company, set up in 1836 in Cork Street, not too far from the Guinness brewery. The company built the first Geoghegan-designed loco in 1882, producing a further seventeen until 1921. Remarkably, these were the only locomotives the company ever built.

The design of the track was equally innovative: the gauge was a mere 1' 10" and the layout of the track within the brewery was designed to work with points and only one turntable. Special wagons were designed, suitable for such tasks as carrying hops and malted barley to the brewhouses. Low level bogie wagons were used for the wooden casks that were used for transporting the products of the brewery and for other items such as bagged hops.

The steam locos lasted until the introduction of Hibberd diesel locos in the late 1940s and those served until the railway was closed in 1975. One of the old Spence-built steam locos and a diesel loco are on display, in perfect condition, in the transport gallery in the Guinness Storehouse, which details the history of the company's railway system.

Geoghegan also devised the means for linking the two levels of the Guinness brewery. The upper and original part at St James's Gate is about 40 feet higher than the lower level, used for such activities as cask making. The initial means of linking the two levels was with a hydraulic lift, but this meant that the wagons had to be uncoupled, a time consuming task. Geoghegan found inspiration in the Gotthard railway tunnel in Switzerland and he adapted the design to the Guinness site. The result was a tunnel beneath James's Street that enabled complete trains to travel between the two levels of the brewery by means of track laid in a spiral fashion. This spiral portion was on the upper side of James's Street under the narrow gauge locomotive shed and before the straight bit of the tunnel beneath James's Street (see map page 2). Geoghegan also devised the signalling system so that the tunnel could be worked in complete safety. Indeed, the Guinness railway was so robustly designed and operated that it never experienced a serious accident.

Some other features were equally ingenious. Guinness put a safe on wheels and on Fridays, traditionally pay day, this was taken by rail to certain parts of the Guinness site so that workers could be paid. Guinness also had a small number of two-axle open cars with roof awnings that were coupled to steam locos to take visitors on tours around the brewery, anticipating the development of similar tours at tourist sites around the world. The most famous visitor to take a trip on one of the Guinness tourist trains was Queen Victoria during her visit to Ireland in 1897, one of the four she made during her reign.

Geoghegan's ingenuity wasn't confined to the railway. About ten years after the railway was constructed, it was decided to build a broad gauge 5' 3" line, conforming to the Irish standard gauge, to link the lower yard within Guinness to the goods yard at Kingsbridge station. The line was built, like a tramway, into setts along St John's Road, passing along the way what was then Dr Steevens' hospital and nurses' home, since demolished, which was right beside the track. At first horses were used to draw wagons to and from Kingsbridge, but Geoghegan designed a unique form of convertor wagon to run on the broad gauge rails. Four of these wagons were built and into each a Spence narrow gauge steam loco was lowered. The motion from the Spence locos was transmitted to the wheels of the convertor wagon, thus providing propulsion for the goods wagons going to and from the Kingsbridge goods yard. The first locomotive for the broad gauge line was built in 1912; it was petrol-driven and only lasted in service for four years. In due course, two broad gauge steam locos were designed and built and they remained in use, alongside the convertor wagons, until the line along St John's Road was closed.

The old Dublin Corporation had never been a great fan of the St John's Road line; even when it was being proposed the corporation was hostile to the idea. But it was only as traffic volume along the road started increasing that the corporation finally got its way when the broad gauge line was closed in 1965.

Close by where the broad gauge line exited the lower yard of Guinness was yet another unique part of the brewery's distribution system. For many years Guinness barges were loaded with full casks of stout at the quayside on Victoria Quay. These barges then made their way downriver towards the Custom House area of the River Liffey, where the casks were transferred to much larger vessels for shipment to Britain. As the barges went under the bridges on the River Liffey, so too were their funnels lowered. For many years the Guinness barges were a familiar Dublin sight and the railway system was extended from the lower yard to the quayside

A view of the Guinness sidings at the Kingsbridge station goods yard, probably taken in the late 1970s and showing a gantry crane for unloading casks as well as more modern forms of transport: a CIE diesel loco, a VW pickup van and a motorcycle.

so that casks could be brought straight to the barges. The system of using barges to take casks downriver ended in 1961 as more modern forms of transportation had come into use.

Most of the locos, wagons and other artefacts from the Guinness system were sent for scrap, first following the broad gauge closure in 1965, then after the narrow gauge closure in 1975. However, some locos have survived – see the following section. Some of the tramway lines can still be seen embedded in the setts in the streets of the Guinness brewery, including on the approaches to the Guinness Storehouse. Inside the Storehouse is an impressive display of relics from the tramway system, as well as the Guinness Archives, which hold documents relating to the system. Guinness meanwhile continues to be as innovative as ever, with the latest development being a new whiskey distillery, which is planned to start production in 2019, with its first distilled whiskey on sale in 2022. Samuel Geoghegan wouldn't have been in the least bit surprised.

Preserved locomotives and rolling stock from the Guinness railway: where are they now?

Narrow gauge steam locomotives built by William Spence and Company:
No. 13, built 1895, acquired in 1956 by the Narrow Gauge Railway Museum, Talyllyn, Wales.
No. 15, built 1895, located at the Irish Narrow Gauge Trust (INGT), Cavan & Leitrim Railway Museum, Dromod, Co. Leitrim. Missing its boiler but otherwise complete.
No. 17, built 1902, originally preserved in the old Guinness museum within the brewery complex, but moved to the Guinness Storehouse in 2002.
No. 20, built 1905, acquired in 1956 by the old Belfast Transport Museum in Witham Street and subsequently moved to the Ulster Folk & Transport Museum, Cultra, Co. Down.
No. 21, built 1905 and given to an employee of the Guinness brewery in 1975; currently located at a private site in Co. Galway.
No. 22, built 1912, now in the Stradbally Steam Museum, Main Street, Stradbally, Co. Laois. This loco has the boiler from the Spence-built locomotive No. 15.
No. 23, built 1921, now in the Amberley Museum and Heritage Centre at Arundel, West Sussex, along with one of the Guinness convertor wagons and the gantry lift used for lifting narrow gauge locomotives in and out of the convertor wagons.

Narrow gauge diesel locomotives built by F. Hibberd Ltd, Park Royal, London (all built to 1′ 10″ gauge; No 35 was regauged to 2ft):
No. 25, built 1947 (the first diesel loco made for Guinness), currently being restored at the INGT/Cavan & Leitrim Railway Museum, Dromod, Co. Leitrim.
No. 31, built 1950, now at the INGT/Cavan & Leitrim Railway Museum.
No. 32, built 1950, acquired for the Guinness Storehouse in 2001.
No. 35, built 1950, located at the Ulster Folk & Transport Museum, Cultra, Co. Down. It was regauged in 1979 to 2′ gauge so it could be used on a small demonstration railway at the museum.
No. 36, built 1950 (the last diesel constructed for the Guinness brewery). Currently under restoration at the INGT/Cavan & Leitrim Railway Museum.

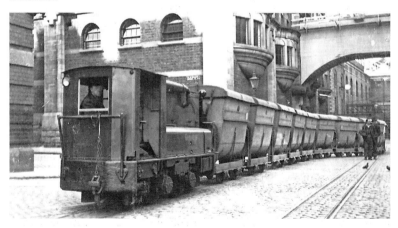

Spence loco No. 23. Described as a 'spare loco', it didn't run well and was only used in an emergency. It is pictured outside the narrow gauge locomotive shed.

No. 32 of the Hibberd diesels in action in Robert Street, close to the malthouse, in 1951. The tipper wagons are full of hops being taken to the brewhouses.

Broad gauge steam locomotive built by Hudswell, Clarke & Co., Leeds: 0-4-0ST (saddle tank) engine No. 3BG, built 1919. It was withdrawn from service at the Guinness Brewery in 1965 and presented that same year to the Railway Preservation Society of Ireland. The original livery was green but it is now dark blue, the Gunness house colour. The loco now carries the nameplate 'Guinness', from the last diesel locomotive, No. 4, also built by Hudswell, Clarke & Co.

Rolling stock (all four coaches built by Ross & Walpole, Ringsend, Dublin):
Visitor coach No. 1, on display at the Ulster Folk & Transport Museum.
Visitor coach No. 2, privately preserved in Co. Galway.
Visitor coach No. 3, in storage at the Ulster Folk & Transport Museum.
Visitor coach No. 4, on display at the Stradbally Steam Museum.

Hop wagons, Nos. 1–4:
All preserved at Cavan & Leitrim Railway Museum, these wagons were originally used to convey hops from the Guinness Grand Canal harbour to the stores. At some stage in the 1950s they were transferred to the engineering department in Guinness and used for maintenance purposes, as well as for track repairs. Three of the wagons ended their days at Guinness by being used in the carpenter's workshop, without motive power, for carrying timber and other items along an isolated section of track. Two of the wagons were regauged at Stradbally to three feet, while the other two kept their narrow gauge.

Grain tipping wagons:
Three of these wagons survive, one built by W. Allen & Co., Birmingham, the other two built by Ross & Walpole in Dublin. Two of the wagons are at the INGT/Cavan & Leitrim Railway Museum, while the third, built by Ross & Walpole, is on display in the Guinness Storehouse.

Safe wagon:
The wagon on which the safe was bolted was made by Hislop & Co., Glasgow, while the safe was made by Avery. It's preserved in store at the Guinness brewery, for eventual display either as a loan item or on display in the Guinness Storehouse.

Snow plough wagon:
Builder unknown, preserved at the Guinness brewery.

Standard gauge vans:
Guinness once had a selection of vans for use on the standard gauge, 5' 3", railways in Ireland. Five special porter vans, all bogie vehicles, were built for use on the GNR(I) railway and attached to passenger trains as required. One of these vans has survived and is on static display at the RPSI headquarters in Whitehead, Co. Antrim.

Guinness also once had a fleet of 20 bulk bogie grain vans which were used to take specially malted grain from Belfast Docks via the GNR(I) to the brewery in Dublin. The surviving van has a built-in grain hopper inside, with sliding roof sections to allow for loading from a grain elevator. This van is currently being restored at the RPSI headquarters at Whitehead, Co. Antrim, for exhibition purposes. This van was built at the Great Northern railway works in Dundalk in 1895; all the other vans were also built there.

Transporting the cash for wages was one of the more unusual purposes of the Guinness railway. Every Friday, pay day, sirens sounded on the roof of the front offices and on the power station, a signal for all the gates to the brewery to be closed. A safe was bolted onto a special bogie and taken from the main cash office in the front yard and towed through the tunnel beneath James's Street. The money in the safe was paid to men working at the lower level of the brewery, in the cooperage sections and in the traffic and racking departments. Five minutes after the first siren, a second blast on it indicated that the cash had reached the lower level cash office and that the gates could be safely reopened. The cash train operated for many years until 1962, but the siren on the power station still sounded until the late 1990s.

The brewery yard, *c.* 1906. By this time the railway had been operational for close on 30 years, construction having been completed by 1877 with the line extending to eight and a half miles inside the brewery. Initially, the rails were made from iron but they were soon upgraded to much stronger steel. Much of the railway had been constructed before Samuel Geoghegan was appointed head engineer at Guinness in 1875, although he did supervise the construction since its inception. When he joined the Guinness staff in 1872, he already had extensive overseas engineering experience, gained in places as diverse as England, Egypt, India and Turkey. It was one of the Guinness family, Arthur Ernest, who had spotted Geoghegan's prodigious talent and recruited him to the brewery.

The brewery yard pictured in 1890 and showing the only turntable that operated on the narrow gauge system. This was sited outside the narrow gauge locomotive running shed. Despite the advent of the tramway system nearly 20 years previously, horse drawn carts are still very much in evidence here; they had also been the sole means of motive power on the broad gauge line to the Guinness siding at Kingsbridge railway station until 1888. At the time this photograph was taken, Guinness was using a total of nine narrow gauge steam locos and close on 200 wagons, both tipping wagons (designed by Samuel Geoghegan) and flat bogie wagons. Some 120 bogie wagons in all were purchased by Guinness for transporting such materials as completed barrels and bagged goods. By the mid 1890s the narrow gauge tramway was handling about 1,500 tons of traffic each working day. The track layouts were designed for easy movement. To give an example of how the system worked, a locomotive with nine empty bogie wagons would leave the cask washing sheds, then go to the cask repairing shed where it would leave one empty wagon and hook on in front a loaded wagon before travelling to the cooperage. There it would leave one empty wagon and collect a full wagon, and would carry on like this through the various yards and loading banks. Speed was slow since the trains rarely moved faster than walking pace and certainly never exceeded ten miles per hour.

Altogether in this photograph, taken in the brewery yard in 1906, seven of the eighteen Geoghegan-designed locos built by Spence are visible. The building behind the turntable is the narrow gauge locomotive running shed and the loco on the right is pulling a hops train.

A view from the lower yard of the Guinness Brewery, 1948. The narrow gauge tramway was linked to the Guinness siding in the goods yard at the Cork or 'country' end of number one platform at Kingsbridge station, now Heuston station, by a standard broad gauge line. In 1874 Guinness had petitioned for permission to build the line, which was originally worked by horse power; horses towed two wagons at a time. Then in 1890 and at the request of Guinness, the Great Southern & Western Railway included in their parliamentary bill that year the right for the line to be worked by steam, despite the opposition of Dublin Corporation. Samuel Geoghegan had already introduced another of his innovations in the spring of 1888. Existing narrow gauge locomotives were lifted onto a wagon which transmitted the drive from the wheels of the narrow gauge locos to the broad gauge wheels on the track. The first of those convertor trucks cost £450. Until 1888 the broad gauge line's sole motive power was horse-drawn, but that year the first two gantry cranes were installed to haul narrow gauge locos in and out of the convertor trucks. Another gantry was installed in 1893 and the last in 1903.

The Corporation eventually had its way when the railway line along St John's Road, beside Kingsbridge station, was closed down because of increasing volumes of road traffic. The rail link was closed down in May 1965 and replaced by a tractor/trailer road service. The name of the station was changed to Heuston the following year.

The closure had been scheduled to take place on Friday 14 May 1965, but at the last moment it was postponed until the next day even though at that stage Guinness had been working a five-day week for many years. Two trains were made up of nineteen wagons each, loaded with returned empties, and hauled by No. 2 loco with No. 3 loco on standby. The last day of the broad gauge service drew quite a crowd and the cab of the loco was filled with people, so much so that the driver remarked 'room on top only'.

Today, the old Dr Steevens' Hospital is an administrative centre for the Health Service Executive and an extensive open grassed area, which was once the site of the hospital's nurses' home, lies between the building and St John's Road. But when the Guinness broad gauge railway was operational the line ran right past the front of the nurses' home (see page 45).

No. 2 steam loco on the broad gauge line on the last day of service in 1965. The first loco for the broad gauge line was built in 1912 by Straker-Squire, London. It was a strange looking contraption, a four cylinder petrol-mechanical engine, and its many drives and shafts required so much maintenance that it only stayed in service for four years. The first steam loco built by Hudswell, Clarke of Leeds was delivered in 1914, the second in 1919; both were engines of conventional four wheel saddle tank design. Just as diesel locos eventually ousted steam on the narrow gauge tramway, the first broad gauge diesel loco, also built by Hudswell, Clarke, was delivered in 1949. While Guinness owned the locomotives used on the broad gauge railway line, the wagons used were owned by the various railway companies, then by CIE which took over the country's railways in 1945. All the steam locos used on the broad gauge line had to meet strict legal requirements; each locomotive had to have a metal skirt fitted before it could be used along St John's Road. Another requirement for working the broad gauge line was having a man with a red flag walking in front of every Guinness train that used the line; the trains never went faster than walking pace.

A broad gauge loco seen in 1948. If there was a shortage of wagons to transport casks, quite often caused by slow unloading at destination stations, then cattle wagons were used as a substitute. The Guinness yard at the Cork end of Kingsbridge/Heuston station platform No. 1, on the down side, was closed in November 1988 and the operations moved across to the up side of the station yard. This photograph shows the broad gauge tracks being crossed by narrow gauge lines in the Guinness Brewery lower yard.

A plentiful supply of empty wooden Guinness barrels can be seen beside the loco in this 1948 picture, while three of the four convertor wagons are in the background. Note the absence of a bung in at least one barrel.

So that casks could be returned in pristine condition for reuse, the cask cleaning shed was a vital part of the Guinness operation. The trains that collected the empty casks usually hauled nine wagons. Using a total of 27 bogie wagons, one loco driver and his guard could deliver about 8,000 casks to the washing shed during the course of a twelve hour day. Once the casks had been cleaned they were filled at retorts and after bunging were rolled down the rails to the loading loft, where they were labelled and dispatched. Cask making and cleaning was a huge operation, much dependant on the tramway within the brewery; up to 15,000 casks a day could be dealt with. This photograph was taken in 1890.

Wooden cask or barrel making was a huge enterprise within the Guinness brewery for nearly 200 years until March 1963, when the last wooden cask was filled. That event almost coincided with the closure of the broad gauge link to the Guinness sidings in the goods yard at Kingsbridge station. Making the casks from wooden staves was a highly skilled job, the work of coopers, and the wet coopering undertaken at Guinness was the most highly skilled form of cask making. Repairing wooden casks was also a considerable undertaking. In the 1920s Guinness employed around 300 coopers, about half the total then in Dublin, but by 1961 their numbers had fallen to 70. Aluminium kegs started replacing wooden casks in 1946, then just over 40 years later stainless steel took over. With the huge amounts of wood needed for cask making, the transportation of finished casks and then the return of damaged casks for repairs, the Guinness tramway system was vital for ensuring the cask making and repair facilities were well serviced. This photograph from 1930 shows some of the extensive rail system within the cask making shop. That rail system was used both for the delivery of timber and for carting away completed barrels. The sheer size of the Guinness brewery in the 1920s can be judged by the fact that it then had around 4,000 employees, making it the largest employer in Dublin.

The cooperage yard at Guinness, seen in 1906 with a veritable mountain of casks ready for use while one of the narrow gauge locos lets off steam. So many casks were made at the brewery that it's estimated the largest stack of them contained no less than 25,000 barrels. The casks were dispatched by train either to Victoria Wharf or to the Guinness siding at Kingsbridge station. The casks that weren't moved by rail were dispatched from the Guinness Grand Canal harbour. Casks in the Dublin area were delivered by horse-drawn drays. Note the Great Southern & Western Railway wagons in the left centre of the photograph and the Midland & Great Western Railway covered wagons to the right of the building. Both the Great Southern & Western and the Midland & Great Western railways had wagons dedicated to Guinness traffic. The Midland & Great Western fleet comprised two 8-ton wagons built in 1898 and 23 10-ton wagons built in 1916. The Great Northern Railway (Ireland) built twelve 20-ton capacity bogie wagons in 1898 for Guinness traffic.

A panorama of the lower level of the brewery, close to Victoria Quay, with mountains of casks stored, ready for use. Note the horse-drawn drays and the lack of mechanised transport.

The railway system in the lower part of the brewery extended as far as Victoria Quay on the River Liffey. A total of 75 eight-wheeled wagons were used in the lower yard to transport casks to the quayside. At its height, the fleet of river lighters numbered sixteen in all, but by the end of the 1950s this had dwindled to five. The last of the River Liffey barges was withdrawn from service in 1961. Also to be glimpsed in this 1930 photograph, behind the lamp post, is Kingsbridge station.

A loco shunting a train of casks on Victoria Quay in 1955. Originally, a rail link from Victoria Quay to Kingsbridge railway station was planned, but a Dublin city tramway depot, on a site leased from Guinness, was in the way. Instead, a line went from the lower yard, along St John's Road to an entrance to the goods yard at the Cork end of platform 1 and the military platforms, and into the Guinness sidings. The tramway depot was closed in 1927 and relocated to Conyngham Road; a garage was later built on the original site and the rail layout remodelled. As part of the 50th anniversary commemorations for the 1916 Easter Rising Kingsbridge station was renamed after Seán Heuston, one of the Irish Volunteers executed in the wake of the rising.

Wagons laden with casks in the lower yard in 1920. Despite the War of Independence at that time the brewery continued to operate as usual. Note the broad gauge track to the left, with a Great Southern & Western Railway open two-axle wagon, No. 4952.

A photograph of the lower yard taken in 1965, the year before the abolition of the Guinness barges which moored at the adjacent Victoria Quay. Kingsbridge station is visible on the left. During this time there was a change in the way casks were made and a mix of wooden and metal casks can be seen.

A steam loco coming out of the maltstore in Robert Street in 1890, en route to the brewhouse. The loco is one of those from Sharp Stewart, either No. 4 or No. 5, from 1878. Robert Street was one of the first areas of the brewery to have a railway track. The tracks had been laid first for the internal transport of malt, hops and full and empty casks and were later extended outside the brewery to Cornhill, Rainsford and Robert streets. In addition to the Robert Street malthouse, another was built adjacent to Cookes Lane and close to the quays, and the malt was transported from the lower to the upper levels by train. The Robert Street maltstore was designed by architect Robert Worthington and built between 1885 and 1886. Barley was delivered by train, then steeped, floored and kiln dried, with the malting season running from September to May; the resulting malt was emptied into wagons on the tramway system and then transferred to the malt stores. The brewery had a total of 33 mash tuns or kieves, with a total capacity of 7,000 barrels of malt, as well as nineteen boiling vessels or coppers.

Once the malt was ready for use it was transported by train to the breweries; this 1930 photograph shows malt wagons being loaded up. Although Guinness had a considerable fleet of tipper wagons and bogie wagons, few survived the closure of the narrow gauge railway in 1975. A hop wagon can be seen in the Guinness Storehouse, while a couple of small wagons went to the railway at Stradbally and an open carriage went to the Ulster Folk & Transport Museum; otherwise, little survived. In this photograph, note the Doric-style cast-iron fluted columns.

No. 18 by Victoria Quay. The rather threatening looking coupler on the loco is held up by a large linked chain.

Flat bogie wagons being loaded with bales of hops, an essential ingredient in the brewing process, before being transferred to the breweries. This photograph was taken about 1930. A total of 208 four-wheel tip wagons were used on the Guinness railway; each weighed three-quarters of a ton and had amazingly large capacity, 80 cubic feet. They were designed so that the centre of gravity allowed one man to release a catch and tip the body to the desired side, left or right. Other bulk loads transported by the wagons included malt and spent grains .Two types of wagon were in use, four-wheel side tippers and eight-wheel bogie flats. The side tippers were by far the most numerous. The wagons were carefully designed to create the maximum capacity and fit the loading gauge; the extreme sharpness of the curves on the lines in the brewery – some had a mere twelve foot radius – meant that only a three-foot wheelbase could be used. Initially, perishable loads such as hops or malt were protected by tarpaulins, but later metal lids were used. A coupling system unique to Guinness was used, with drag hooks mounted on the locos. The wagons all had shackles on the couplers to prevent accidental uncoupling, a system used first on the narrow gauge steam locos and later also on the diesel locos. The Guinness wagons were patented by Samuel Geoghegan and a number of similar wagons designed and patented by him were used to transport stone ballast on the Giant's Causeway electric tramway in Co. Antrim. The first of these tipping wagons came into use in 1887.

The most ingenious part of the railway system in Guinness was the spiral tunnel that connected the two levels in the brewery; the original upper level, off James's Street, was and still is much higher than the lower level. Connecting the two levels by rail provided Samuel Geoghegan with an intriguing challenge. At first, the 40 foot difference between the upper and lower levels was bridged with a hydraulic lift, but shunting trains into single wagons that could be transported up and down on the lift was very time consuming. Geoghegan decided that a spiral tunnel between the two levels, with a gradient of not more than 1 in 40, would be far better. He took his inspiration from the Gotthard railway tunnel in the Swiss Alps and the spiral tunnel was built in 1887/88 at a cost of £3,000.

The first step in the construction of the tunnel was digging a 25-feet-deep circular trench, a tricky operation because part of it went beneath No. 98 James's Street. But the excavation was completed successfully and the inner and outer sides were supported by two concentric circular walls of brick. Between these, a circular brick arch was built, rising from bottom to top like a circular staircase. The radius of the spiral tunnel was set at 65' 3" with 2.65 turns and the aforementioned gradient, although later sources said the gradient was 1:39. The rail length was 864 feet. The tunnel was 7' 3" high and 8' 9" wide. At the top of the tunnel the line connected with the other lines in the upper level of the brewery, while at the lower end the track ran from Victoria Quay to the tunnel entrance in a zigzag incline so that empty trains could easily climb to the tunnel. But like all railway tunnels, after it was completed it leaked water vigorously.

Geoghegan also devised a unique signalling system for the tunnel, based on levers at each end of the section, attached by wire ropes. On entering the tunnel, the train driver pulled a rope attached to the lever, which prevented another train entering the tunnel from the opposite direction. This manual system worked very well for many years, but in 1963 was replaced by a system of electric coloured lights. In the photograph on the facing page note the signalling apparatus above the locomotive. Nowhere else on the Guinness system had formal signalling; flags and hand signals were used as required.

The photograph shows the entrance to the tunnel, while alongside is the entrance to the pedestrian tunnel which ran alongside the spiral tunnel. Jonathan Virden, who worked as a brewer at Guinness from 1961 until 1973, and whose father before him had worked at Guinness in both Dublin and London, recalls a strange story about the tunnel. A pipe ran through the tunnel carrying Guinness. There was a standard time of four minutes for trains to go through the tunnel, but one day an errant driver did the journey in two. An investigation began; the errant driver was teetotal and, allegedly, it turned out that the other drivers had been using a spike in the pipe to extract the Guinness inside so their journeys actually took two minutes longer than necessary. Today, the tramway tunnel is still used for beer mains and the adjacent pedestrian tunnel remains in use.

The Guinness railway had just one turntable, seen here; it was operated by manpower. In order to reduce to a minimum the numbers of wagons used, and to maximise their use, the tramway was constructed with triangular reversing loops. These triangular junctions on the lower levels of the tramway were time saving, as locos did not need to run around their trains of nine bogie wagons. The locos picked up empty cask wagons from the various departments of the brewery, while at the same time leaving behind the same number of empty wagons.

Narrow gauge loco No. 7 on a convertor wagon, preparing to haul wagons to Kingsbridge goods yard. The wagons belonged not to Guinness but to the Great Southern & Western Railway and were noted for their spoked wheels. In the background can be seen the gantry for lowering the locos into the convertor wagons.

One of the four ingenious convertor trucks in action in the lower yard at Guinness, 1906. The building in the distance, on the right of the photograph, is Kingsbridge station, while the building in the middle of the photograph is the nurses home for Dr Steevens' Hospital at the entrance to St John's Road. Today, the road is better known for the headquarters of eir, the telecommunications company. The train seen here was made up mostly of roofless five-ton capacity cattle wagons, which had been in use to transport cattle until 1877 when a government order announced that cattle would have to be conveyed in covered wagons.

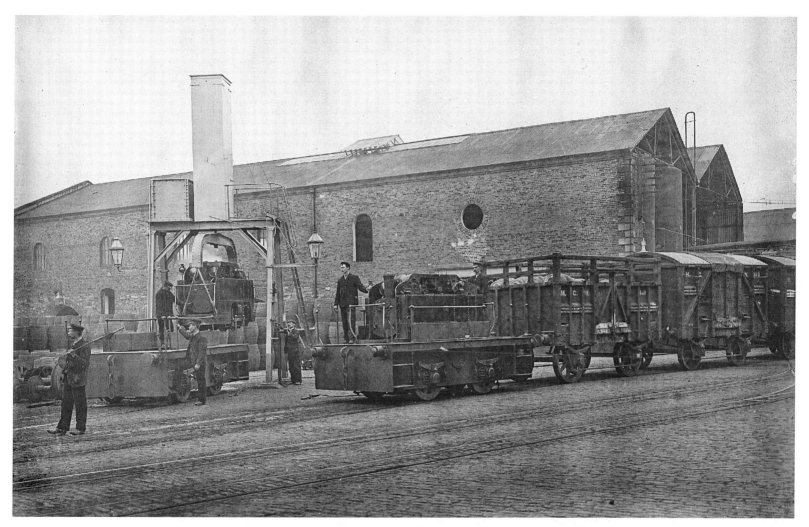

A narrow gauge steam loco swinging precariously from the gantry elevator. The wagons belonged to the old Midland Great Western Railway, which merged with the Cork, Bandon & South Coast Railway and the Great Southern & Western Railway in November 1924 to form the Great Southern Railway. The following year the newly formed railway company was joined by the Dublin & South Eastern Railway to form Great Southern Railways. This lasted until 1945 when CIE assumed control. CIE was nationalised five years later.

Spence locos Nos. 23 and 24 by the lift which hauled them up into the convertor wagons. A total of four convertor wagons were built by Spence between 1888 and 1903.

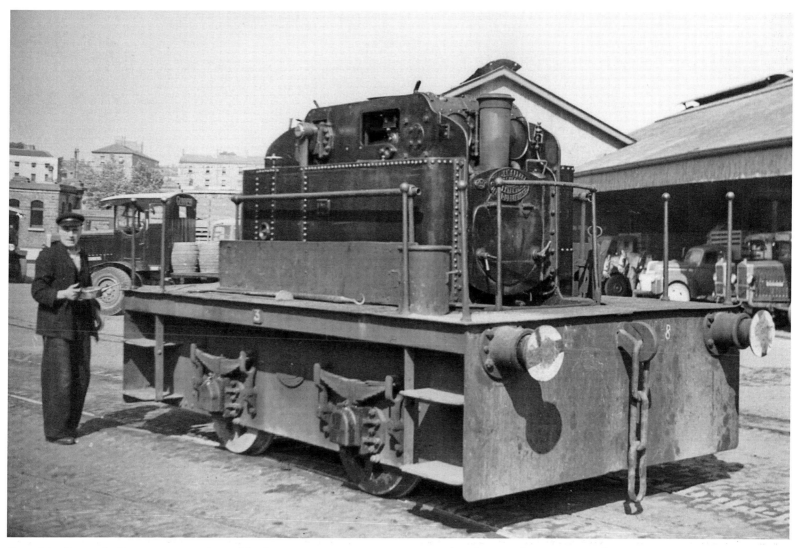

One of the Spence-built narrow gauge locos, No. 17, seen in No. 3 converter wagon. This photograph was taken in the Guinness Brewery lower yard; in the background, to the left of No. 17, can be seen Collins Barracks, now part of the National Museum of Ireland.

One of the last steam locos on the narrow gauge tramway, No. 15, built in 1895 and seen here in the 1950s. The boiler of No. 15 was fitted to the frames of No. 22 in 1956 and it then assumed the new number, 15. After this loco was withdrawn in 1965, it was preserved in Co. Laois. The first steam loco for the system had been built in 1875 by the Avonside Engine Company in Bristol, but its weight and power were inadequate for the loads that had to be hauled. Two further steam locos were purchased in 1876 and appropriately named Malt and Hops. After a total of five locos had been purchased by Guinness, Samuel Geoghegan decided to go one better by designing his own locomotive for the system. The main drawback with the early steam locomotives, apart from the length of time it took to get them ready, was that they picked up dirt and dust very easily from the tracks. So Geoghegan designed a loco that weighed less than seven and a half tons and could haul an 18-ton load up the incline of the tunnel. To counteract the problem of the valve motion being so close to the ground, Geoghegan put the two cylinders and valve motion on top of the boiler. The cylinders drove a horizontal crankshaft from which vertical connecting rods drove the rear wheels. A conventional coupling rod linked the back and front wheels.

The Avonside Engine Company built the first loco to Geoghegan's design at a cost of £848. The prototype worked so well after it was delivered in 1882 that Guinness placed an order with the Spence company in Dublin, even though they had no experience of locomotive building, although they had been very involved in the construction of the narrow gauge tramway a decade earlier. The locos it built for Guinness were very successful, able to haul 75 tons at slow speed on the level and 18 tons up the steepest gradient. These were the only locos that Spence ever made. The firm closed down in 1930. It occupied Nos. 121–123 Cork Street.

The first attempt at replacing the narrow gauge railway came in 1970, when a Ponndorf compressed air system was installed to carry the spent grains from the brewhouse to an area where they were collected by local farmers. The system never worked well because it was too long for the successful use of compressed air. Several mobile compressors were brought in to boost the air power, but they all burned out and vast piles of used grains ended up deposited in the wrong place. It took Guinness another five years to find an efficient system to replace the old tramway; ducts and conveyors were part of the new system, which did work well.

Loco No. 12, built at the Spence works in 1891 and scrapped in 1954. In July 1888 the prestigious Institution of Mechanical Engineers, based in London, held a meeting in Dublin. Some half-dozen topics were covered, including a description given by Samuel Geoghegan of the tramways and rolling stock at the brewery.

Spence loco No. 18 hauling bogie wagons loaded with casks. The locomotive was built in 1902 and used until 1951 when it was scrapped.

A Geoghegan-designed steam engine, made by the Spence company in Cork Street, outside the Market Street storehouse in 1948. Three years later the last of the diesel locomotives was delivered to Guinness. The delays caused by watering the steam locos was one reason for the abolition of steam locos, as well as the laborious process of lighting up, coaling and oiling, then returning to the shed during the day for more water and coal. Then, at the end of the day, the fire had to be dropped and the fireboxes and smokeboxes cleaned out. All a diesel needed was a cursory examination before work started, then the key was turned and away it went. But the diesels didn't provide the seamless all-day working that had been expected and were actually less well suited to the job than their predecessors. The rail traffic in the brewery was inevitably 'stop-go' and this meant that the diesel motors couldn't heat up properly, inhibiting their working at maximum efficiency. However, for working crews the diesels were a big improvement, with cabs enclosed on three sides giving much greater protection from the weather and, even more importantly, the many obstructions in the brewery, such as the chutes in the malthouses. The diesel exhausts weren't as bad as those of the steam locos, which meant that working a diesel train through the tunnel was less noxious for drivers.

A diesel engine pulling a train of low level bogie wagons loaded with bags of hops, 1955. The first diesel loco, made by F. C. Hibberd, was No. 25 in the Guinness fleet, coming into service in 1947. Diesel engine No. 32 can be seen alongside a steam narrow gauge loco in the Guinness Storehouse.

A Hibberd diesel hauling a train of hop wagons in the front yard at the brewery in the 1950s.

A Hibberd diesel with a train loaded with hops in front of the Market Street storehouse, 1948.

In this photograph, taken in the early 1960s, the Guinness tramway and the cars seemed to be competing for space within the brewery. No. 34, one of the narrow gauge diesel locomotives, is hauling a train of tipper trucks laden with hops, while a couple of motor cars jostle for space. In those days Guinness workers often parked their cars beside the kerbs on the streets within the brewery. On one occasion several cars belonging to employees came a cropper. A fully laden train of grains was shunting on icy rails on the western side of the brewhouse when the driver lost control and the train slid down the slope, derailing at the bottom. It crashed into a line of parked cars, destroying several of them and the train broke through the main gates into James's Street. Fortunately, no one was hurt and all the workers who had had their cars wrecked were given new cars by the company.

Diesel No. 34 emerging from one of the malthouses, having just unloaded a train full of barley. The malted barley is mixed with water from Poulaphouca Lake in Co. Wicklow, then it is mashed, after which it goes into mash tuns or kieves, and the grain is separated from the liquid known as sweet wort. The liquor is fermented for several days with brewer's yeast, which turns the sugar into alcohol. It is the malted barley that gives Guinness its characteristic flavour.

Diesel No. 34 in Robert Street, close to the former fermenting house. Also seen in the photograph is a van belonging to McBirney's, a department store based on Aston Quay, on a delivery run to the brewery. McBirney's closed down in 1984. The overhead bridge led from the malthouse, the fermentation building, to an adjacent brewery building. In 1904 Guinness engineers designed three bridges linking what was then the fermenting house to other brewery buildings. Another of the bridges, in Market Street, led from the fermenting house to one of the vat houses. The three bridges had a unique and elaborate lattice design which was later enclosed to give protection against the weather, as seen in this photograph. The bridges were built by a local firm, Ross & Walpole, based in Ringsend. The seven-storey fermenting building was converted into the Guinness Storehouse, which opened to the public in 2000. This has become the most popular tourist attraction in Ireland and attracted over 1.6 million visitors in 2016.

Broad gauge loco No. 2, built by Hudswell, Clarke in 1914. The locos were of a standard design, adapted for the Irish 5' 3" broad gauge. The motion and the wheels of these locos were enclosed with 'skirts' and a bell fixed to the running plate, which were requirements for locomotives working on street tramways.

Another shot of one of the two steam broad gauge locos used to haul casks of stout to the Guinness siding at Kingsbridge station and return empties from the goods yard to the brewery. The photograph shows the loco coming out of the brewery, through the gate onto St John's Road. These two locos were built by Hudswell, Clarke and numbered 2BG (broad gauge) and 3BG to differentiate them from their narrow gauge counterparts Nos. 2 and 3.

No. 4 broad gauge diesel loco leaving the lower yard to make the 500-yard journey to the Guinness siding at Kingsbridge station. There is no clear indication when the line to the railway station opened; some sources say it was as early as 1874, while others say it didn't happen until the 1880s. The line along St John's Road was laid in granite setts, very like a street tramway, and it remained like this until the time of its closure. The rail used was of the centre grooved type, unique in Ireland, which meant that the wagons ran on their wheel flanges instead of their treads. This kind of rail also necessitated an unusual type of points, where the whole rail moved like a stub point. Each of the trains on the broad gauge line consisted of thirteen fully laden wagons. Two of the original converter wagons, with two of the 1921 narrow gauge steam locos, were still working up to the end of the broad gauge system in 1965. The first broad gauge loco was far from successful; it was a four-wheeled petrol driven loco built by Straker-Squire in London in 1912, but it gave a lot of trouble in traffic along St John's Road and was withdrawn from service after just four years, being finally sent for scrap in 1921. Two broad gauge steam locos with saddle tanks were built by Hudswell, Clarke in 1914 and 1919; they worked well for many years. The fourth and final loco built for the broad gauge line was a Hudswell, Clarke diesel, assembled in 1949 and named 'Guinness'. The nameplates on the diesel loco seen here are now carried on Guinness steam locomotive No. 3BG which is in working order at the headqurters of the Railway Preservation Society of Ireland.

Guinness sent a circular to all heads of departments on 14 April 1965, stating that the planned closure date for the broad gauge link from the brewery to the goods yard in Kingsbridge station was 17 May. In preparation for this a shuttle service of eight tractors and 40 trailers was fitted out in the Guinness garage, and a new loading bank was completed at the old jetty siding in the brewery, as well as new loading facilities at the Exchange siding in Kingsbridge goods yard. The sight of locos hauling wagons loaded with full kegs from the brewery to the railway station or returning with empties would finally be a thing of the past. After the narrow gauge tramway ceased operating in 1975, one unnamed worker at Crampton's the builders, who were involved in dismantling the railway, remembered helping to tear down the railway fittings in the brewery and replacing them with a more modern system using conveyor belts and ducts for such products as waste hops. This photograph shows Diesel No. 4 moving at a suitably slow pace past the nurses' home at Dr Steevens' hospital. The railings on the right are at the front of Kingsbridge station.

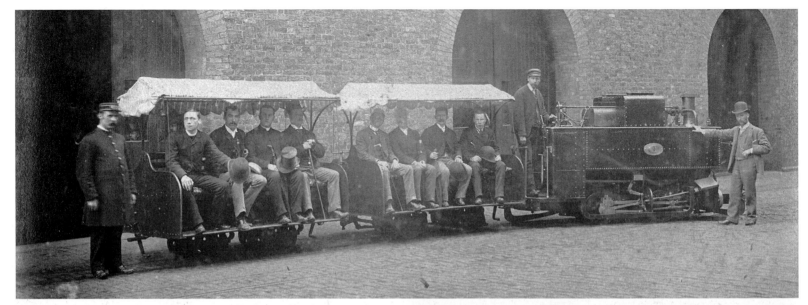

For many years Guinness ran special carriages on its railway network to transport tourists around the brewery. This photograph was taken in 1890; seven years later Queen Victoria visited Dublin as part of her Diamond Jubilee celebrations and took a trip on the Guinness tourist train. The narrow gauge steam loco seen here, No. 4, was built by Sharp Stewart, Manchester, in 1878 and was in service until 1925 when it was scrapped.

For many years the tourist train was hauled by the first loco built for the narrow gauge railway. This 1875 Sharp Stewart 0-4-0 two-ton saddle tank cost the brewery £445. It proved unsatisfactory at hauling wagons and was swiftly consigned to hauling the tourist train, which it did until it was withdrawn in 1913. This loco had been ordered by a man called Strype, the Guinness engineer before Samuel Geoghegan. Its main disadvantage was that the working cylinders, valves and motion were very near the ground and so picked up dust, sand and dirt very easily, causing parts to wear out prematurely. This prompted Geoghegan to design locos that had these vulnerable parts placed on top of the boiler, using vertical coupling rods.

The Guinness tourist train was very popular with visitors long before the Guinness Storehouse was thought of. Its specially designed carriages enabled visitors to sit 'side saddle' while they were protected to some extent from the elements by overhead awnings. The tourist train had wooden slatted seats, as well as wooden ledges for visitors to rest their feet on. Four people sat on one side of the carriage, while another four sat back to back. This photograph was taken in 1949 and the loco seen here, No. 12, was built by Spence in Dublin in 1891 and survived until August 1954 when it was scrapped.

Diesel No. 31 with a tourist coach, complete with canopy. This locomotive was built by F. C. Hibberd in 1950 and is seen here later in the decade. This loco is now preserved at the Cavan & Leitrim Railway Museum, Dromod.